Author's Note

From the early 1900s into the 1960s, blue whales were hunted to near extinction for baleen, oil, blubber, and meat. More than 360,000 whales were killed.

In 1966, blue whales became a protected species through a global ban on whale hunting. Nevertheless, blue whales remain few in number and are still threatened by many things, such as collisions with ships, destruction of habitat, pollution, and entanglement in commercial fishing gear.

Blue whales are magnificent and intelligent creatures, and like all of the natural world they deserve our admiration and care. It is only then that they will flourish and multiply in their native ocean homes.

This book is dedicated to Amy Wiggin.

-J.D.

We gratefully acknowledge Diane Gendron of CICIMAR (Interdisciplinary Research Center in Marine Science, based in La Paz, Baja California Sur, Mexico, affiliated with the National Polytechnic Institute) for her expertise on blue whales and her passionate and exacting commitment to this book.

www.enchantedlion.com

First edition, published in 2015 by Enchanted Lion Books,
351 Van Brunt Street, Brooklyn, NY 11231
Text and Illustrations copyright © 2015 by Jenni Desmond.
www.jennidesmond.com
A CIP record is on file with the Library of Congress. ISBN 978-1-59270-165-0
Printed in China in December 2014 by the South China Printing Co.
1 3 5 7 9 10 8 6 4 2

THE
BLUE
WHALE

JENNI DESMOND

ENCHANTED LION BOOKS
NEW YORK

Once upon a time, a child took a book
from a shelf and started to read.

He read that the blue whale is a mammal
of gigantic size and strength. It is the
largest living creature on our planet.

A blue whale can measure up to 100 feet. That is the same length as a truck, a digger, a boat, a car, a bicycle, a motorcycle, a van, and a tractor—all lined up.

A blue whale's heart is the largest of any animal. It is as big as a small car and weighs about 1,300 pounds.

Blue whales are gray but they look bright blue underwater, which is how they got their name. Their skin color ranges from dark to light gray and is mottled like marble. It feels smooth, rubbery, and slippery to the touch. A blue whale's underbelly sometimes appears yellowish-white. This happens when microorganisms called *diatoms* attach themselves to it.

Every blue whale has unique markings, similar to our fingerprints. Scientists use these, along with the shape of the dorsal fin, to identify individual whales.

An average blue whale weighs around 160 tons, or about the same as a heap of 55 hippopotami. Females grow bigger and heavier than males. This is because the female cares for her baby on her own and needs to be big enough to produce enough milk to feed it.

No land animal can be as big as a blue whale because no bone structure can be strong enough to support such colossal weight out of the water. The salt in seawater helps keep these huge whales buoyant. Seawater gives buoyancy to all other creatures too, like hippopotami and humans.

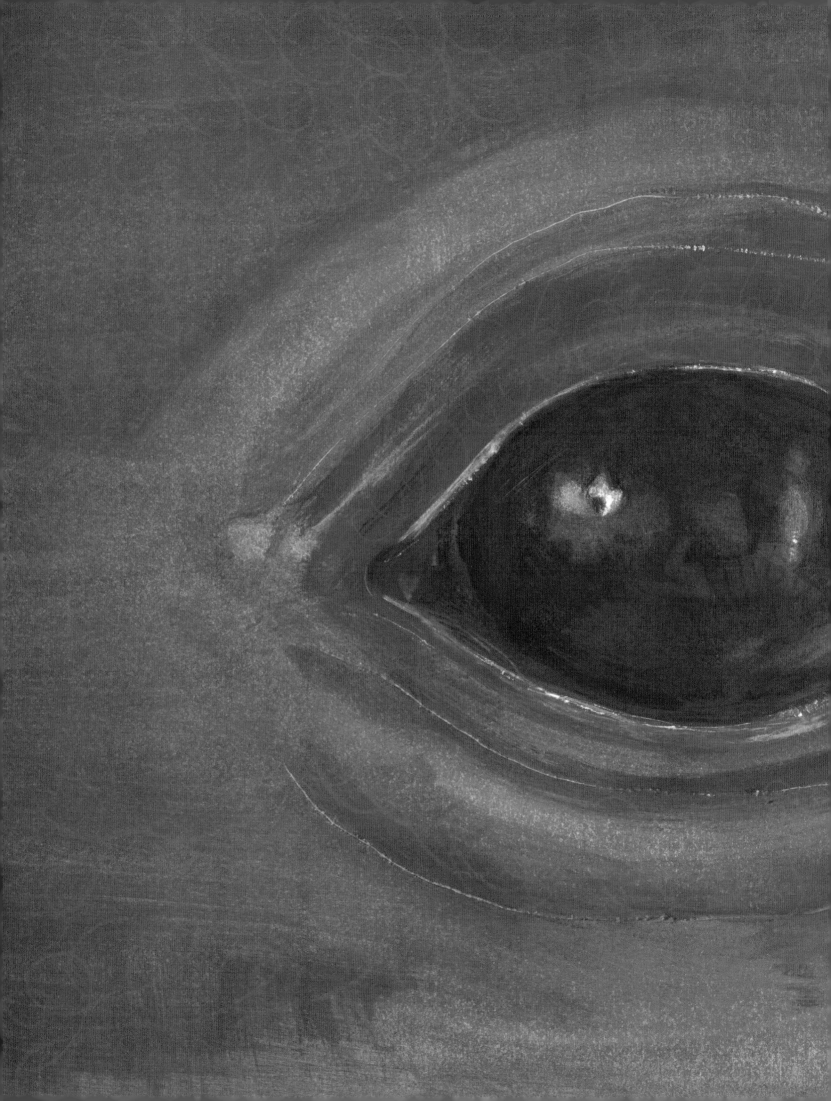

A blue whale's eye is about six inches wide and has no tear glands or eyelashes. It is very small, considering the size of its body. Blue whales have poor eyesight and a poor sense of smell and taste, but their hearing is excellent and their skin is highly sensitive.

BALEEN PLATES

The top of a blue whale's mouth is lined with 300–400 baleen plates, which are made of a black fingernail-like material. A blue whale's tongue weighs three tons, and its mouth is so big that 50 people can stand inside it. Fortunately, blue whales don't eat people.

Blue whales eat mostly krill, a tiny shrimp-like creature. During the summer months, they eat about 35 million krill each day, which is about four tons of food. But since they have narrow throats, they can swallow only a grapefruit-sized amount at one time.

Blue whales eat different species of krill, depending on the ocean in which they live.

To eat, the blue whale takes a giant
gulp of seawater and krill. It takes so
much water into its mouth that the ventral
pleats below its jaw and belly expand, like a huge
accordion.

When the blue whale is ready to swallow,
it pushes all of the seawater back out of its
mouth with its tongue through its bristly baleen
plates. These plates catch the krill for the whale
to swallow. Because krill are bright orange, so
too is a whale's poo.

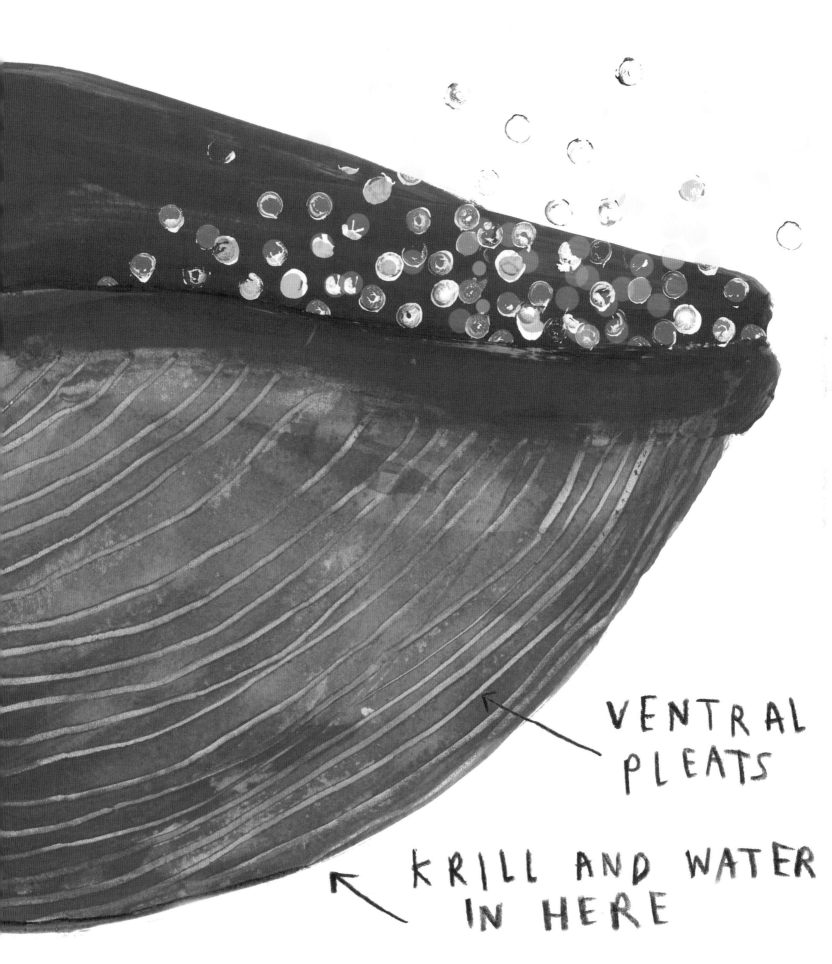

VENTRAL PLEATS

KRILL AND WATER IN HERE

Baby blue whales don't eat krill; they drink their mother's milk. A baby blue whale is called a calf, and its mother, a cow. The calf is in its mother's womb for almost a year and is about 20 feet long when it is born. It drinks nearly 50 gallons of its mother's milk every day and can gain as much as nine pounds an hour. By eight months, the calf will start to feed itself by eating krill.

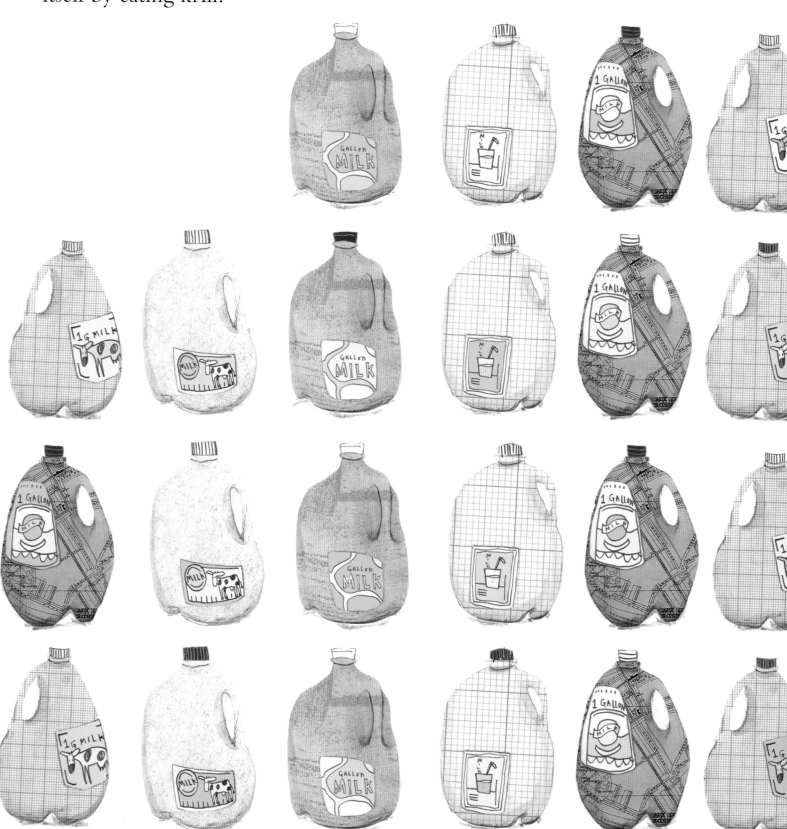

Blue whales have approximately the same lifespan as that of humans. Today, scientists are able to determine a whale's age by tracking it from birth using photographic identification. Scientists used to identify a blue whale's approximate age by using the waxy earplug found inside its ear canal. Just as we can tell the age of a tree by counting the rings of its trunk, scientists could figure out the age of a whale by counting the bands of wax that had built up over time. This method could only be used on captured whales, however, so it was eventually abandoned as unethical, as well as unreliable.

Blue whales aren't able to breathe underwater, but they can hold their breath for up to 30 minutes, depending on their activity. When they come up to the surface for air, blue whales exhale through two nostril-like blowholes, blowing air as high as 32 feet (the height of nine seven-year-old boys). A single breath could inflate 2,000 balloons. The sound of a blue whale blowing is thunderous and can be heard up to several miles away.

Blue whales are graceful, streamlined swimmers. Each side of its tail is called a fluke, and together these two flukes measure about 18 feet (the wingspan of a small plane). Flukes move up and down like a bird's wings, not side-to-side like a fish's tail.

Blue whales also have a small triangular dorsal fin on top of their backs and two short, tapered flippers. Together, these help them to steer.

A blue whale's ears are located near its eyes and are tiny little holes. Despite this, blue whales have excellent hearing. This is important because they have to be able to hear each other in the ocean across great distances. Their song is louder than a jet engine and can be heard up to 1,000 miles away. They are one of the loudest animals in the world, but the frequency of their sound is too low for humans to hear it without the use of equipment.

The blue whale's song resembles a foghorn and vibrates through the water with pulses, moans, and rumbles.

Sound is important to blue whales for both communication and navigation. It guides them through the ocean towards food and helps them find a mate. However, the noise coming from ships and other man-made vessels is often so loud that it interferes with marine life and can even confuse a mammal as large and loud as the blue whale.

NORTH
AMERICA

NORTH
PACIFIC
OCEAN

NORTH
ATLANTIC
OCEAN

EQUATOR

SOUTH
AMERICA

SOUTH
PACIFIC
OCEAN

SOUTH
ATLANTIC
OCEAN

ARCTIC
OCEAN

Blue whales have been found in all the oceans
of the world. There are three subspecies
of blue whale: the Pygmy Blue Whale, the
Northern Hemisphere Blue Whale, and the
Antarctic Blue Whale. Most blue whales feed
on krill during the summer months and then
migrate to warmer areas near the equator for
the winter, where pregnant females give birth.

EUROPE

ASIA

AFRICA

PACIFIC
OCEAN

INDIAN
OCEAN

AUSTRALIA

SOUTHERN
OCEAN

ANTARCTICA

Blue whales sleep by taking very short naps while slowly swimming close to the ocean's surface. This is called *logging*. They sleep in this way because they have to remember to open their blowhole in order to breathe. Blue whales can never completely lose consciousness, not even in sleep, otherwise they would drown.

Unlike blue whales, people can drift into sleep without having to remember to breathe and keep themselves afloat, so we can fall asleep over a favorite book and begin to dream...

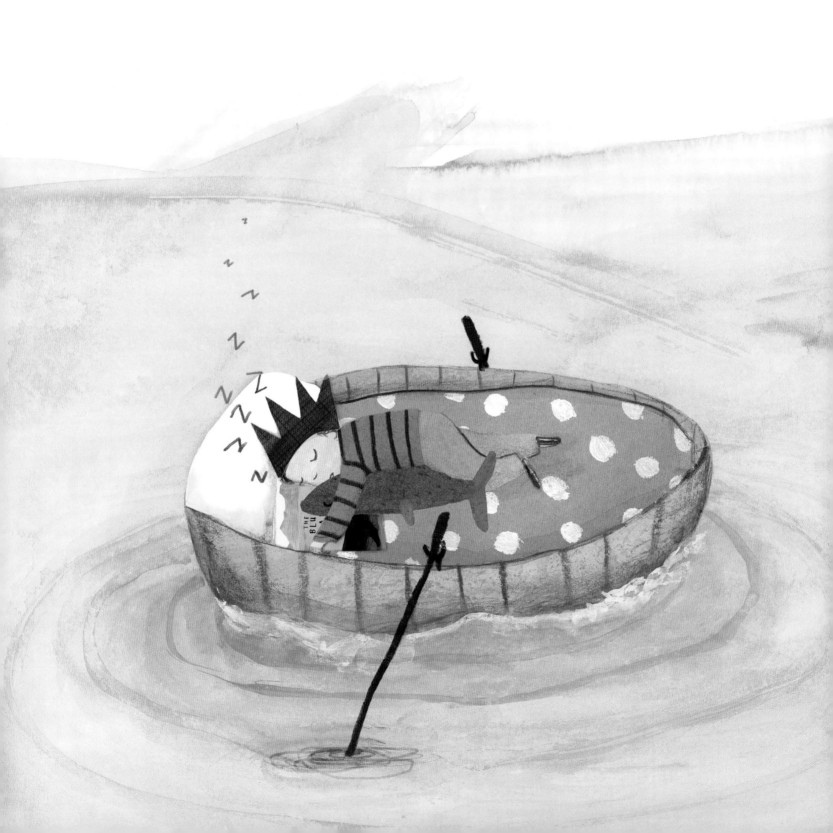

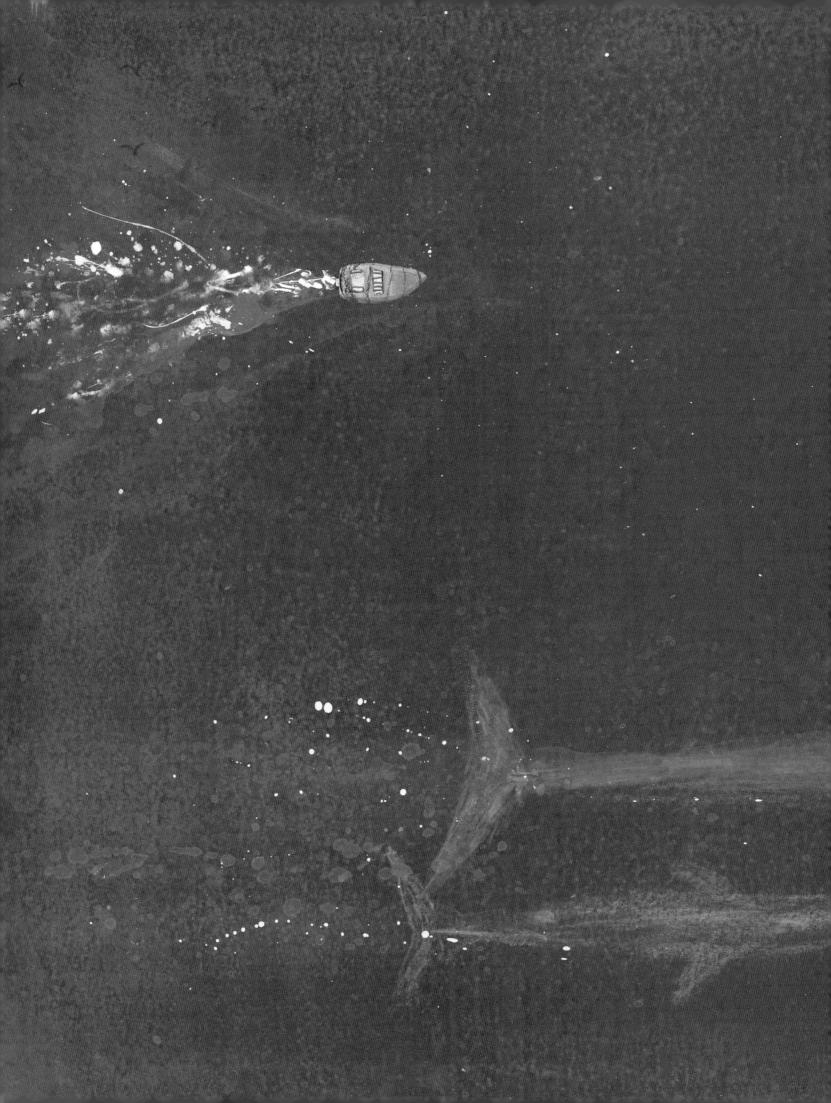